INTO
Wild Brazil

**BLACKBIRCH®
PRESS**

San Diego • Detroit • New York • San Francisco • Cleveland • New Haven, Conn. • Waterville, Maine • London • Munich

For more information, contact
The Gale Group, Inc.
27500 Drake Rd.
Farmington Hills, MI 48331-3535
Or you can visit our Internet site at http://www.gale.com

LIBRARY OF CONGRESS CATALOGING-IN-PUBLICATION DATA

Into wild Brazil / Elaine Pascoe, book editor.
    p. cm. — (The Jeff Corwin experience)
Based on an episode from a Discovery Channel program hosted by Jeff Corwin.
Summary: Television personality Jeff Corwin takes the reader on an expedition to observe wildlife in the Pantanal, a wetlands ecosystem in western Brazil that is home to the largest river otter, snake, and rodent.
Includes bibliographical references and index.
  ISBN 1-56711-853-4 (hardback : alk. paper) — ISBN 1-4103-0175-3 (pbk. : alk. paper)
  1. Zoology—Brazil—Juvenile literature. [1. Zoology—Brazil. 2. Brazil—Description and travel. 3. Corwin, Jeff.] I. Pascoe, Elaine. II. Corwin, Jeff. III. Series.

QL242.I58 2004
591.981—dc21   2003009281

Printed in China
10 9 8 7 6 5 4 3 2 1

E ver since I was a kid, I dreamed about traveling around the world, visiting exotic places, and seeing all kinds of incredible animals. And now, guess what? That's exactly what I get to do!

Yes, I am incredibly lucky. But, you don't have to have your own television show on Animal Planet to go off and explore the natural world around you. I mean, I travel to Madagascar and the Amazon and all kinds of really cool places—but I don't need to go that far to see amazing wildlife up close. In fact, I can find thousands of incredible critters right here, in my own backyard—or in my neighbor's yard (he does get kind of upset when he finds me crawling around in the bushes, though). The point is, no matter where you are, there's fantastic stuff to see in nature. All you have to do is look.

I love snakes, for example. Now, I've come face to face with the world's most venomous vipers—some of the biggest, some of the strongest, and some of the rarest. But I've also found an amazing variety of snakes just traveling around my home state of Massachusetts. And I've taken trips to preserves, and state parks, and national parks—and in each place I've enjoyed unique and exciting plants and animals. So, if I can do it, you can do it, too (except for the hunting venomous snakes part!). So, plan a nature hike with some friends. Organize some projects with your science teacher at school. Ask mom and dad to put a state or a national park on the list of things to do on your next family vacation. Build a bird house. Whatever. But get out there.

As you read through these pages and look at the photos, you'll probably see how jazzed I get when I come face to face with beautiful animals. That's good. I want you to feel that excitement. And I want you to remember that—even if you don't have your own TV show—you can still experience the awesome beauty of nature almost anywhere you go—any day of the week. I only hope that I can help bring that awesome power and beauty a little closer to you. Enjoy!

Best Wishes!
Jeff

INTO
Wild Brazil

NORTH
AMERICA

EUROPE

ASIA

Atlantic
Ocean

Pacific
Ocean

AFRICA

SOUTH
AMERICA

Indian
Ocean

Pacific
Ocean

AUSTRALIA

Brazil is a place where giant rodents swim alongside giant reptiles. There are grasslands, rivers, lagoons, and flood forests—a vast wetland ecosystem with many habitats, where all sorts of creatures live.

I'm Jeff Corwin.
Welcome to Brazil.

Brazil is home to the world's largest rodent—the capybara.

Motoring in the Pantanal...

I'm Jeff Corwin, and I want to welcome you to Brazil—not to the teeming cities or famous beaches, but to a wild wonderland called the Pantanal.

The Pantanal spans about 84,000 square miles of terrain, an area roughly the size of New England, in western Brazil. It's sandwiched in between Brazil, Bolivia, and Paraguay. And I'm right in the middle of it, on the Pichain River, one of several rivers that snake across this plain. Along this river we can see all kinds of animals— birds like bitterns and herons, snakes, capybara, caimans, and even tarantulas. But there's one creature that draws us to this river habitat. It's one of the rarest creatures living in South America.

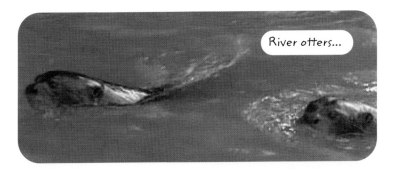

River otters...

...the largest in the world.

Look at those eyes!

Look at this—we have two giant river otters, the largest otters in the world, and incredibly rare. Check out the size of these animals. Giant river otters can measure 6 feet in length and weigh up to 80 pounds. Amazing animals, extremely intelligent, they are close relatives of the mink.

These otters have webbed feet, which help them swim. They are superb fishers, the master predators on this river. Match an otter to a caiman, and the otter will win every time. In fact, otters eat caiman.

I've heard you can actually attract these animals if you whistle, mimicking their call. And it's true—I've drawn a whole pod.

These animals look cute and cuddly. But do not underestimate their power, because when pressed, they can be very protective.

Giant river otters, a great treat. It doesn't get any better than this, even with all the mosquitoes here. And they're just one example of the wildlife that is waiting to be discovered here in the Pantanal of Brazil.

That forked tongue picks up scents.

Oh, my gosh. Right in front of me a huge serpent has come to the river's edge—a yellow anaconda, the largest snake you'll find in the Pantanal. I'm so excited, I'm shaking. And it looks like the river otters are excited, too. I think they might want to take this snake from me.

These snakes are powerful constrictors. When the anaconda is in hunt mode, he tracks his prey down with that flickering forked tongue, which is his way of picking up scents. He reaches out and strikes to secure his prey, whether it be a baby capybara, some sort of waterfowl, or another creature. He then coils around his prey and, each time the prey exhales, the snake squeezes tighter and tighter, until the animal he is constricting suffocates. Then the snake swallows his prey whole.

These yellow anacondas can grow 12 or 13, sometimes even 14 or 15 feet in length. While they are the largest serpents in the Pantanal region, they're somewhat dwarfed by their cousins to the north, the green anacondas. The green anaconda grows nearly twice as long as the yellow. Still, you don't need anything much longer than this baby, if you want to see what a big snake looks like up close and personal. We'll let the anaconda go back to the hole where he lives.

Do you see the caiman?

Shhh! Quiet.

Caimans love these grasslands because they can blend right in among the tall vegetation and murky water—which, by the way, is also full of flesh-eating piranha. We've come up on a caiman that's very large, about 7 feet in length, and since it's not totally submerged I have a pretty good chance at capturing it. The trick is to lay something over its head, so it can't see. These animals

With its eyes covered, a caiman goes limp.

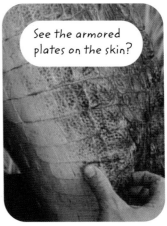

See the armored plates on the skin?

depend almost entirely on visual cues, and without sight they're shut off from the world and just go limp.

With his eyes covered, I can pick him up, and we can get a good look at him. He's a gorgeous specimen. Look at the size of this guy—a huge spectacled caiman, *Caiman crocodilus*, or Jacaré, with is a regional term for alligator.

Webbed feet for swimming...

You can see these creatures are well armored. They have scutes, armored plates, throughout their skin, even over the stomach. That armament protects the animal's rib cage and his stomach from any predators that would want to eat him. And look at his feet—he has wonderful webbed feet for swimming, and a powerful tail that he uses for defense and propulsion.

...a powerful tail for defense.

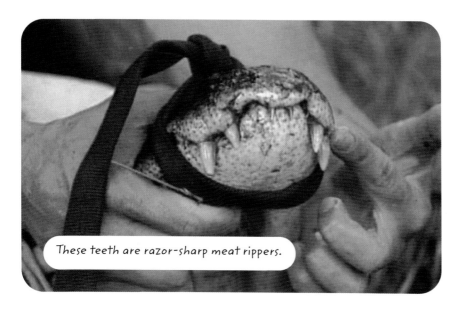

These teeth are razor-sharp meat rippers.

Razor-sharp teeth hang all the way around this creature's jaws, a deadly array. When this creature hunts, he bites onto his prey and then rolls in the water. The more the prey struggles, the more he fights to secure his dinner. And what's neat is that when he dives underwater, his nostrils close up so that he doesn't take a lot of water into his lungs.

How do you let go of a caiman that doesn't like you? You let go quickly!

Capybaras are so cool.

This big guy is a capybara, the largest rodent in the world. "Capybara" means "masses in the grasses," and these animals are masses in the grasses and the water here. Capybaras are extremely social, so it's not very common to find an individual hanging out in a solitary fashion like this. This is probably an adolescent male, weighing about 90 pounds. Someday, he might hit 180 or 200 pounds.

Capybaras are herbivores, which means they eat vegetation. The one I'm looking at is illustrating that for us by chowing down on some water hyacinth. You can find capybaras all the way through South America. They often live in herds, and often the younger ones are separated into a nursery where a capybara

These are social creatures.

Capybaras have webbed feet.

All these animals live in the water.

matron keeps watch over them. They're beautiful creatures, excellent swimmers and divers with webbed feet.

Capybaras are an important source of food for many animals in this part of the world. Jaguars and pumas eat capybaras. Young capybaras fall prey to anacondas, and large capybaras like this fall prey to creatures like the caiman.

In fact, while I've been trying to sneak up on this capybara, five or six caimans have moved in. It's a great illustration of the circle of life—the omnivore (that's me) wants to check out the herbivore, but the carnivores are coming to check out the omnivore. I think we'll move along.

This is the Transpantaneira Road.

Found a porcupine...

The Transpantaneira Road stretches 80 miles between the north and south points of the Pantanal. Right now it's in excellent condition, but in the rainy season it will be flooded and bridges will be washed out. I'm going to follow this road for a few miles and find a good area for exploring.

Just off the highway, I've spotted a prehensile-tail porcupine, a really interesting animal with a great defense. I've followed it at least 20 feet up this tree, and now it's at the very end of this branch, just out of reach. We've raised a camera into the tree, and despite the fact that I'm being eaten by ants, I am going to film this porcupine so you can have a look at it.

This is not an aggressive animal. It's an herbivore that spends most of its time in trees. Actually, it was probably sleeping here through the night. But when a stupid predator, like myself, comes along and tries to grab it, a pincushion of pain awaits. Those quills are tipped with barbs.

This porcupine is smaller than the ones that we see in North America. Its quills are coarser and more blond or two-toned in color. And it has a prehensile tail, which can grasp branches. These creatures are masters at climbing, and they're very comfortable up in the treetops. They have claws that they use to pull themselves through the branches, as well as that tail, which functions as a fifth limb.

These quills are mighty dangerous.

These critters use their tails to climb.

I hope you don't have arachnophobia—because if you do, you're not going to want to hang around with this guy. This beautiful creature is a tarantula. Although it is, for the most part, harmless to people, for small animals it's a different story. As with most species of spiders, the tarantula is venomous. It has a set of fangs to the front, which are literally extensions of what were once limbs or digits.

I'm being very careful with this guy.

Now, why isn't this tarantula biting me? That's a great question. The reason is because I'm being careful. I'm keeping my hands still, letting them be like part of the environment that the animal normally crawls across. If I make any sudden movement, it will react. And even in that case, it probably wouldn't bite me unless I really hurt it.

The tarantula's fangs are for the most part reserved for securing prey. It grabs onto its prey, such as a cockroach or a lizard or even a small rodent or bird, and sinks those fangs in, injecting the prey

This one's actual size—just kiddin'!

21

Back to his little home.

with venom. The venom not only immobilizes and kills the prey, but it also promotes digestion. The prey actually dissolves into something like a spider frappe or milkshake, and then the tarantula just drinks it up.

Let's place this creature right back underneath its log, and we will continue our search for other wonders of nature.

I'm a pantanero!

I've stopped at one of the many cattle ranches you'll find in the Pantanal. Cattle ranching is big business here, and the cowboys—or *pantaneros* as they're called locally—take pride in managing their land.

These are togo toucans, one of my favorite South American birds. They are juvenile birds, only a couple of months in age, and the story is that they were orphaned and are being hand-reared by the people that run this ranch. I'm hoping that when these toucans are ready to live on their own, they'll have the opportunity to live free again. But right now, it gives us a nice chance to see something up close that you rarely get to experience out in

These are togo toucans.

Look at that yellow...

These are still young birds.

nature. See how this bird holds his large yellow bill? That's what you do when you're a baby toucan and you want your mother to feed you. If my fingers were the bill of this creature's parent, out would come a nice, slurpy, regurgitated soup of fruit and insect parts.

These guys are greedy—they're eating up a bunch of fruit.

Sorry, no food here...

Here's my parrot call...

Hyacinth macaws are the world's largest parrots.

Out of the approximately 340 species of parrots living on our planet, these hyacinth macaws are the largest. They're also the rarest. There are only 3,000 of these gorgeous birds left in South America. And you only find them in this region, in Bolivia and in Brazil.

This group of macaws has flown here to feed on one specific type of food, a hard-shelled palm nut. With their powerful bills, they're the only parrots that have the ability to crack this nut open and extract the fatty tissue in the center. They're specialists—this is pretty much the only stuff they're going to eat, and it's all that stands between them and extinction.

Macaws pair up for life.

Macaws are monogamous birds; male and female bond for life. And these creatures are excellent parents. They invest a lot of their energy in securing a future for their offspring. It's not uncommon for a hatchling, as it develops, to stay with its parents within a flock for up to a year and a half, even two years.

These are huge birds, nearly 3 feet in length from the tip of the head to the end of the tail, with a wingspan of nearly 4 feet. Their beautiful plumage is violet in color, and if you look around their eyes you'll see a fleshy cup of bright yellow skin.

As we all know, there are many endangered species on our planet. But to lose this gorgeous species of bird would be a great loss to natural history and a great loss to us. There are a number of reasons why this animal is close to extinction. Reason number one: loss of habitat. Keep in mind, these birds are specialists that rely on these palm nuts, and without the palm trees they will die. Reason number two: These animals are hunted. They're hunted for the black market pet industry because just one of these birds can sell for $10,000 to $12,000. They're also hunted for their flesh and for their plumage. All these reasons come together to push this creature toward extinction.

These birds are so beautiful.

The hyacinth macaw alone is a good enough reason to come explore the Pantanal. But you know me, I'm selfish—I want it all. And there's a lot more to find. Even though some of the area around this ranch has been cleared for cattle grazing, there are still large pockets of natural habitat.

The anaconda of South America is the largest known snake. It holds the world's record for size—the largest one ever recorded measured more than 34 feet in length. And that's just the one that was found—many people are convinced there are even bigger anacondas out there.... These members of the boa family can live in fresh water and—like all snakes—they're carnivorous. Because the anaconda's weight is usually supported by water, it can grow larger than snakes that make their homes in trees. While some snakes use venom (poison) to kill or paralyze their victims, the anaconda, like its Eastern Hemisphere cousins, pythons, kill by constriction. Large anacondas feed on deer, pigs, caiman, and fish—swallowing everything whole. The snake usually wraps its extended jaws around the head of the victim and works its way down to the victim's feet, swallowing as it goes.

I thought this was a baby anaconda...

...but it's another kind of water snake.

And look at this—a beautiful snake. Now, when I first looked at this serpent, I thought it was a baby anaconda. It has a very broad head, stout body, even the coloration of a green anaconda, but it's not. It's a neotropical water snake. Like anacondas, this is a serpent that is comfortable in the water; but it's not a constrictor. It has excellent camouflage, with colors of brown and gray and a bit of olive that go great with that algae and all that mud. The snake sort of sinks into the mud and water, and the only thing that you can see are those eyes, which are right on the top of its head. If you're looking for frogs, you want to be built just like this.

Seeing a creature like this gives you a little clue to the way nature works. To come face to face with such a beautiful animal, and to learn about its natural history in a way that is as non-invasive and as nonintrusive as possible, is a wonderful thing.

Mosquitoes everywhere!

Here's what really stinks about nature, though, at least in the Pantanal: the mosquitoes! Also the stinging ants. *El estúpido*, Jeff Corwin, just put his hand on a plant with stinging ants. Each bite is like a wasp sting.

But up ahead, the trees are swaying. Let's find out what it is...

Up in that tree...

It's a band of howler monkeys, moving into the area. We'll have to be quiet, because these animals are quick to spook. They're

...just howlin' away.

Howler monkey

My vocal cords are nowhere near as powerful as a howler monkey's.

named for their loud calls, which can carry for miles through the forest. The calls are a way to establish territory between one howler monkey troop and the next. They're also a way to ward off predators. The call tells predators, "I see you, you can't eat me."

But the monkeys don't need to worry very much about predators here. Between the stinging nettles, the continuous shower of bird guano from the trees, the mosquitoes—and, of course, the stinging ants—these guys are all set. They don't need any protection. Let's move on and see what else we can find.

If you look quickly at this wonderful creature, you may think it's some sort of crocodilian, like a caiman. It's very caiman like, and it is a reptile, but it's not a crocodilian. It's a caiman lizard, a lizard that is built very much like a caiman. Look at his tail, very crocodilian. But that face is like the face of a monitor lizard. And out of its mouth comes something that's very serpentlike, a forked tongue.

Can you see the lizard in there?

This guy is a crocodilian.

This caiman looks like a little croc.

This caiman lizard is one tough, ancient-looking reptile. He's standing his ground, huffing and puffing at me. When you look beyond that fierce complexion, though, you have to appreciate his reptilian beauty. Look at those eyes, bright black. And the scales along his lips are perfectly aligned. Beautiful lizard.

So, what was he doing? He was foraging around, looking for frogs, for fish, perhaps for the eggs of a bird. This lizard is an excellent

The locals think this creature is half caiman and half snake.

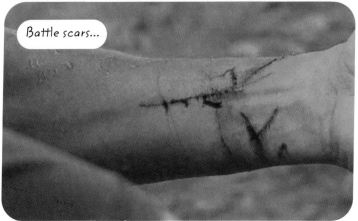

Battle scars...

hunter. The local pantaneros refer to this lizard as *bibola*. They believe it to be very dangerous, half venomous snake and half caiman. The truth is it's harmless. If you leave this creature alone, it's not going to hurt you at all. Of course, if you're an idiot like me and roll around with it, it can put up quite a fight. I've earned some scars from this encounter.

Here's something else interesting about this lizard.

This guy is a survivor.

Adios.

He's missing a hand, but he's functioning fine. He's an adult, around ten years old, and he'll be around maybe for fifteen more years. And he has survived, probably since his early years, minus one hand.

I'll let him go. We have a long trip ahead—800 miles to the port of Itanhaem, and then another four and a half hours by boat to the island of Queimada Grande. Why are we going there? Here's a clue. I'm bringing a supply of antivenin.

Queimada Grande, off the southern coast of Brazil, is the only place on earth where you can find the deadly but beautiful golden lancehead viper. There are no white sandy beaches surrounding this island. As if the deadly snakes weren't enough of a deterrent, the interior is protected by a slippery, jagged shoreline.

Our first discovery on this island isn't a golden lancehead, but a

Coming up on the island.

beautiful little fledgling—a baby booby, probably about a month old. Check it out. It's just sitting there, looking at us, trying to disappear, and hoping we won't approach. The parents of this bird are right on the other side of this bluff. Boobies nest all along these scrapes, which you see along the bluffs, cliffs, and hillsides of the island. There are hundreds and hundreds of these birds living here.

Look at this baby booby.

A rocky, jagged coastline greets you at Queimada Grande.

Hot, humid, and uninviting— excellent!

Got one. A golden lancehead.

Away from the shore, the temperature's pushing toward 100 degrees Fahrenheit, and the humidity is up there as well. This is a very uninviting place. But it's in the dense patches of forest on this island that we'll have the best chance of finding a golden lancehead.

Right between the leaves of a bromeliad I've

These vipers are quick to strike.

found the snake we're looking for. I've had to be really careful catching him because, wow, is he feisty! As long as they are left alone, vipers like this by nature like to mind their own business. The problem with these snakes is that when they're pressed or when they feel threatened, they are quick to struggle, quick to strike.

I'm holding this guy very carefully.

See the distinctive head.

I don't want to be bitten by this snake, and I also don't want this snake to injure himself—he could do that easily by puncturing his own flesh with those two very large fangs in the front of his mouth. I'm using my fingers to prevent that. I've got my thumb and middle finger on either side of the jaw, and I've got my index finger supporting his head, but he's really moving around a lot.

By the way, although I've described how I've held this snake, that's not an instruction for you to go capture your own snake!

I'm afraid he's going to injure himself, so I'm going to let him go. And that's OK because there's another one right here. This island is crawling with snakes. This one is tasting the air with his tongue, picking up our scent. I wonder what it's like be a snake, with a tongue that tastes the world.

These guys are good climbers..

He's rattling his tail as a warning. But unlike its relative the rattlesnake, this viper doesn't have a rattle. Instead he relies on the leaves and sticks around him on the ground, flicking with his tail to make a sound when he feels alarmed.

Look, no rattle!

LOOK AT THIS!

Did you know that the venom composition inside a snake's body can vary throughout its life? It can even vary at different times of the year, and between species." In some  cases, a snake's venom will have more than 130 components. And each component will have a different physical effect on the human body. Venom comes in all kinds of toxic "flavors": Some venom is hemotoxic, which means it poisons the blood; some venom is myotoxic, it attacks muscle; and some venom is neurotoxic, it attacks the nervous system, which will shut down such vital functions as breathing. So which kind of venom is the worst? It all depends how you define "worst." The neurotoxic venom of smaller species of rattlers, such as the Mojave and the Aruba Island rattlesnake, can kill at much lower doses than those from other snakes. But as for pain and suffering and a prolonged recuperation phase, the big western and eastern diamondbacks' venom is the winner. Its venom is very efficient at breaking down (digesting) muscle and skin—which hurts.

So what can save someone from a toxic snakebite? The only thing that helps: antivenin — ideally administered intravenously in a hospital setting. Antivenin arrests deterioration, but doesn't reverse it. That's why fast treatment is critically important.

44

So here's the great million-dollar question. How did the golden lancehead vipers become residents of this island? To find the answer, you have to go back to a time twenty thousand years ago, when this island was a part of the mainland. Then the sea rose, sepa-

This island is a fascinating laboratory at evolution.

rating this little patch of earth from the coast. And when that happened, a population of vipers was isolated. For thousands of years, they've been breeding among each other, closed off from the mainland group. And that has allowed them to evolve into a totally unique species.

There's something else that I find fascinating about this snake, and it's going to blow you away. The females of this species have evolved a male sexual organ called a hemipenis. At this point in their evolutionary history, it's not functional. They can't use it for anything. But perhaps in ten thousand years, it will be functional. And when you have one individual that is able to reproduce on its

Good-bye, Brazil.

own, that's all you need to create a new population. Maybe a snake will drift on a floating log to a neighboring island and establish a new population. That's how one random mutation can change the history of a species.

Obligado. That means "thank you" in Brazil, and I owe a great thanks to this nation because—well, just think of the adventure we've had. From the flood plains of the Pantanal to this remote, lush island, Brazil has provided us with some of the best wildlife encounters I have ever had. And what a great way for us to wrap it up, with an amazing encounter with the golden lancehead. I'll see you on our next adventure.

Glossary

antivenin the antidote for a snake's venom

arachnophobia fear of spiders

caiman a type of crocodilian

carnivores animals that eat meat

crocodilian a type of reptile, such as a crocodile or alligator

ecosystem a community of organisms

evolution Charles Darwin's theory to explain how species adapt and change over time

extinction when no more members of a species are alive

habitat a place where animals and plants live naturally together

hemotoxic venom that damages blood and tissue

herbivores animals that eats plants

myotoxic venom that damages muscle

neurotoxic venom that damages the nervous system

omnivore an animal that eats meat and plants

predators animals that kill and eat other animals

prehensile the ability to grasp or wrap around

propulsion forward movement

reptiles cold-blooded, usually egg-laying animals such as snakes and lizards

scutes bony plates or scales, such as on a turtle's shell

serpents snakes

venom a poison used by snakes to attack their prey or defend themselves

venomous having a gland that produces poison for self-defense or hunting

viper a type of venomous snake

wetland land that naturally contains water and moisture

Index